World Issues

EUTHANASIA

Clive Gifford

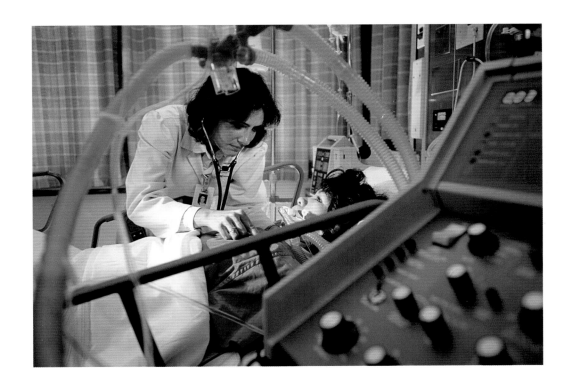

Chrysalis Education

WORLD ISSUES

ABORTION
ANIMAL RIGHTS
ARMS TRADE
CAPITAL PUNISHMENT
CONSUMERISM
DRUGS

EQUAL OPPORTUNITIES
EUTHANASIA
FOOD TECHNOLOGY
GENETIC ENGINEERING
GENOCIDE

HUMAN RIGHTS
POVERTY
RACISM
REFUGEES
TERRORISM

Distributed in the United States by
Smart Apple Media
2140 Howard Drive West
North Mankato, Minnesota 56003

ISBN: 1-59389-156-3

Library of Congress Control Number: 2004043609

Editorial Manager: Joyce Bentley
Editor: Clare Lewis and Joe Fullman
Project Editor: Jon Richards
Designer: Ben Ruocco
Picture Researcher: Lorna Ainger
Educational Consultant: Lizzy Bacon
Americanizer: Margaret Parrish

Produced by Tall Tree Ltd, U.K.

Printed in China

Picture Acknowledgments
The Publishers would like to thank the following for their permission to reproduce the photographs:
Alamy: Steve Allen front cover, 34, Yoav Levy 5, 16, Peter Marshall 32, Photo Network 10,
Popperfoto 29, Shout 21
Corbis: Bettmann 27, 30, Despotovic Dusko/Sygma 47, Ronnie Kaufman 8-9, Kevin R Morris 15,
Liss Steve/Sygma 42, Tom Stewart 14
Courtesy of Exit: 48
Getty Images: 35, 45, Evan Agostini 46, Paula Bronstein 17, Michael Crabtree 11, 24, Richard Ellis 26,
David Friedman 36, Sandy Huffaker 9t, Hulton Archive 23, Patrick Kovarik 9b, Franco Origlia 31,
Adam Pretty 37
Lookat Photos: 22
PA Photos: Deutsch Press-Agentur 18, 19, EPA 6, 25, 38, 39, 44, Johnny Green 49, Chris Ison 13,
Martin Rickett 41, ChrisYoung 28
Photocall Ireland: Gareth Chaney 9c
Rex Features Ltd: Sipa Press 43, 50, Skyscans 33, UNP 40
Science Photo Library: John Greim 20
Still Pictures: Markus Dlouhy 12
Topham: 51

CONTENTS

Petta's Story

Petta is 78 years old and suffers from ALS, also known as Lou Gehrig's disease or motor neurone disease. This is a disease that causes the nerve cells in the brain and spinal cord to deteriorate and the body's muscles to grow weak and waste away. At present, it is an incurable disease which, in most cases, leads to paralysis and death, usually from an inability to breathe. Petta is in the advanced stages of the disease and is considering the possibility of euthanasia.

"**M**Y NAME IS Petta. I was born in Denmark, although I now live in the Czech Republic. I suffer from ALS, have lost the ability to move, and need to be cared for all the time.

I can just about still speak, but that ability will go in the not-too-distant future. My doctor treats me to make sure that I am not in any great pain and that my mind is still alive, but my body feels as if it were dead. My condition has deteriorated so much that I am now past the point where I am able to take my own life.

While I have any strength left at all, I am trying to talk to the members of my family about someone taking my life for me. However, my family is against euthanasia and each of them has different reasons for opposing it. My younger brother is very religious and feels that it is against the will of God as well as the teachings of the Bible. My sister, on the other hand, says that having survived a war, I should know how precious life is.

If I were healthy, I could take my own life, but because I need help from someone, it is a big issue and against the law. As a young man, I fought to survive during World War II, but I now face a battle I cannot win and one that I no longer want to fight. Don't I have the right to die or should I be respecting the views of my loved ones?"

The impact of Euthanasia

The right for a person to choose the time and manner of their own death is creating many debates and issues.

UNITED STATES
Anti-euthanasia campaigners gather to protest in the United States. Here, powerful pressure groups on both sides of the issue are locked in a battle to try to win the full support of the public and the government.

IRELAND
Mourners gather at the funeral of Rosemary Toole, an Irishwoman whose death was assisted by an American minister, the Reverend George Exoo. Reverend Exoo now faces extradition from the US back to Ireland to face charges of assisting a suicide (see page 12).

FRANCE
Jacques Chirac, who, as French President, refused an appeal by Marie Humbert to allow her son Vincent to die. Vincent had lost the use of his limbs as well as his sight, speech, smell, and taste in a car crash (see page 50).

What Is Euthanasia?

The word euthanasia comes from two words in the Greek language: **Eu** *means "well" or "good" and* **Thanatos** *means "death." In modern society, euthanasia now means much more than a "good death." It has come to mean the intentional end of a person's life to end suffering.*

ALL PEOPLE DIE eventually and most die of natural causes when their bodies, due to age, illness, or injury, cease to function well enough to keep them alive. Euthanasia shortens the lifespan of a person by killing them before nature runs it course. Euthanasia can occur by an action, such as when a person's death is caused by giving them a lethal injection of drugs or putting a pillow over their nose and mouth and suffocating them. It can also occur through withholding food and water or through not performing normal and necessary medical care.

Why is intention important?

Euthanasia is to deliberately perform an act or to deliberately not do something with the clear intention of causing someone's death. Without intention to kill someone, euthanasia does not occur. For example, doctors are sometimes faced with a patient who is close to death. They may decide to stop a particular treatment because it no longer has any benefit to the patient's health or they may not start a new treatment because it will not improve the patient's condition. Some groups argue that these are examples of passive euthanasia, but the

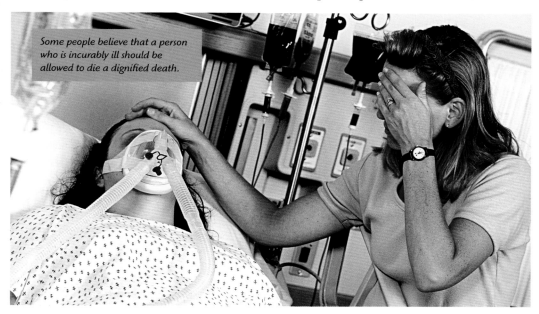

Some people believe that a person who is incurably ill should be allowed to die a dignified death.

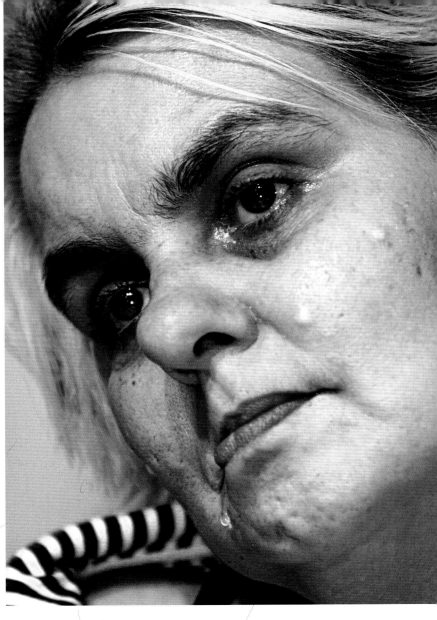

UK resident Diane Pretty suffered from motor neurone disease and campaigned to have her husband help her to die.

general opinion is that these are part of fair medical practice, and these practices are allowed by law in most countries. Since there is no intention to kill the patient, they are not considered to be euthanasia.

What is the double effect?

The double effect, or dual effect, describes how an action can have more than one effect, both good and bad. In particular, it is used to describe the practice of giving a dying patient high doses of certain powerful painkilling drugs to control pain and ease suffering. All drugs have side effects and in trying to control a patient's pain or another symptom, there is the chance that the side effects of the painkilling drugs may weaken the patient and bring about death more quickly. This is generally not considered as euthanasia as, again, there is no deliberate intention to kill the patient, but an attempt to alleviate his or her suffering.

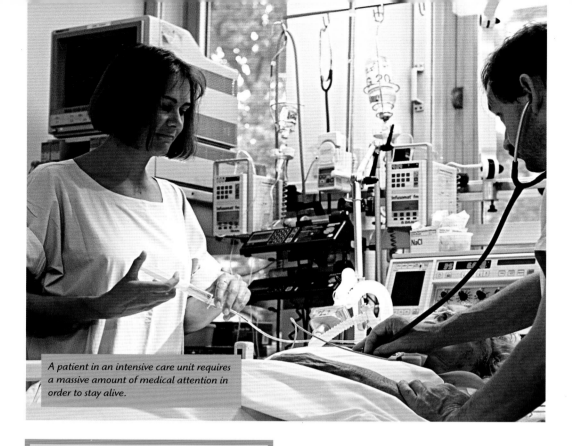

A patient in an intensive care unit requires a massive amount of medical attention in order to stay alive.

Minister assists in the suicide of an Irish woman

An American minister, George Exoo, admitted that he assisted in the 2001 suicide of an Irishwoman, Rosemary Toole. Exoo put a plastic bag over her head and tightened it. He then pumped helium through a pipe running into the bag. In Ireland, assisting a suicide is a serious crime, incurring up to 14 years in prison.

Sources: BBC News and *The Observer*

What is the difference between voluntary and involuntary euthanasia?

Voluntary euthanasia is when the person who is killed has made a specific request for that to happen. In some countries where euthanasia is legal, this request has to be made a number of times by the patient and over a period of time. In contrast, involuntary euthanasia is used to describe the killing of a person who has not clearly expressed the wish to die. Involuntary euthanasia has occurred with patients who have no ability whatsoever to communicate their wishes to carers, doctors, friends, or relatives. These include patients whose conditions have deteriorated to the extent that they are in a type of deep, prolonged coma that is referred to as a persistent or permanent vegetative state, or PVS (see page 28).

Aren't euthanasia and suicide the same?

No. The two are not considered the same in the laws of most countries or in arguments about morals and ethics. Suicide is the intentional taking of one's own life. The final act does not involve anyone else helping in any way. In wealthier, more developed nations around the world, suicides are a significant cause of death. In the United States, for example, the Centers for Disease Control report that, in 2001, there were more deaths from suicide than from murder and that suicide was the eighth leading cause of death for all Americans. The situation is similar in the UK, where the nonprofit organization the Samaritans reported that 5,188 people took their own life in 2001.

The death and funeral of a person is a traumatic time, and some people feel that the prolonged suffering of the person prior to death can add immensely to the emotional pain of those close to them.

DEBATE—Is there a difference between assisted suicide and suicide?

- Yes. The two are fundamentally different. Suicide is a private act and is not against the law in many countries; assisted suicide involves someone else helping to take a life and is illegal in almost all countries.

- No. The end result is the same. A person who wants to die, dies. Does it really matter that someone else was involved in the process?

Many people believe that a person making a living will is unaware of the implications of his or her decision—a decision they may be unable to reverse when the time comes.

What is assisted suicide?

Assisted suicide is when a person provides the means for someone to commit suicide but leaves the final act to the person who dies. When a doctor assists, it is known as physician assisted suicide. Who actually performs the final action, the action which causes death, is what separates assisted suicide from euthanasia. If the person who dies performs the last act, such as the swallowing of a lethal drug supplied by a doctor, then it is classified as assisted suicide. But if a doctor injects a person directly with a lethal drug, then it is euthanasia. While suicide is no longer illegal in most nations, assisted suicide remains a serious crime in nearly all countries of the world.

What is a living will?

A living will is a legal document that sets out how someone wishes to be treated should they become unable to communicate with their doctors. Living wills cannot enforce euthanasia but they can instruct a medical team not to prolong life artificially by giving antibiotic drugs to fight an infection or connecting someone to a life-support machine. Many people argue that living wills give a patient peace of mind by making clear their wishes and taking pressure away from doctors, friends, and family. Critics, however, wonder how it is possible or right to make a decision now for some unknown problem that may or may not occur at some point in the future.

Young people and children may feel that the issue of euthanasia is something they don't have to think about.

I am young. Why should I be interested?

The majority of children in more developed countries, such as the US and the UK, can look forward to half a century or more of life ahead of them. As a result, death as an issue of importance can seem far removed. Surveys reported in the book, *A Right To Die*, indicate that 90 percent of 19 year olds never think of death in relation to themselves, while 70 percent of 65 year olds do. Yet, death affects everyone, sooner or later, and many young people face it directly by being a victim of an accident or terminal illness, or through a dying friend or family member.

An assisted suicide practitioner explains its difference to euthanasia

"It's like giving someone a loaded gun. The patient pulls the trigger, not the doctor. If the doctor sets up the needle and syringe but lets the patient push the plunger, that's assisted suicide. If the doctor pushed the plunger, it would be euthanasia."

Dr. Jack Kevorkian in *Doctor Assisted Suicide and the Euthanasia Movement* 1994

When Did The Euthanasia Debate Begin?

Few subjects arouse more passion and stronger views than life, death, and whether people can choose between them. Debates about rights to life and death have existed since ancient times. However, it is only in the 20th century that euthanasia has truly become a major issue.

PEOPLE IN ANCIENT times tended to live far shorter lives. In the past, medicine was less able to prolong a person's life if they were suffering serious disease or injury. To many historic peoples and cultures, death and life were woven together and part of the natural world. In the aftermath of a battle, for example, people from a number of ancient cultures killed their seriously injured comrades to give them, in their view, an honorable death.

Modern technology, such as this life-support machine, allows us to keep people alive far beyond the time their condition would have killed them in the past.

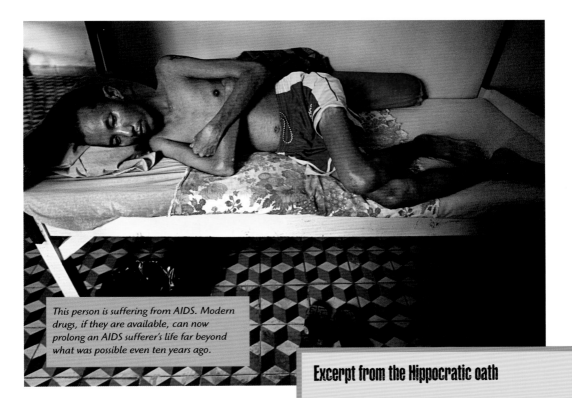

This person is suffering from AIDS. Modern drugs, if they are available, can now prolong an AIDS sufferer's life far beyond what was possible even ten years ago.

What views have been held in the past about suicide and euthanasia?

Views on suicide and euthanasia have varied throughout history. For some Ancient Greeks and Romans, they were considered acceptable. The Ancient Greek philosopher Socrates committed suicide in 399 BC by drinking a cup of poison made from the hemlock plant. Others thought it was wrong, among them the Greek physician Hippocrates (460–377 BC). An oath attributed to him is still taken by many doctors. The Hippocratic oath includes concepts such as putting the good of patients above the interests of doctors. It also places emphasis on a doctor's role in striving to preserve life.

The rise of the world's major organized religions, such as Christianity, Judaism, and Islam, dominated thought on these topics for many centuries. These three

Excerpt from the Hippocratic oath

"I will prescribe regimen for the good of my patients according to my ability and my judgement and never do harm to anyone. To please no one will I prescribe a deadly drug nor give advice which may cause his death."

religions and others held human life as sacred and condemned both suicide and euthanasia. For example, the Qur'an, the chief sacred text of Islam, makes clear that life is sacred because it is only Allah who chooses how long each person should live: "No person can ever die except by Allah's leave and at an appointed term." Countries whose populations followed the major religions tended to reflect this viewpoint in law and made euthanasia and suicide illegal.

How have attitudes to suicide changed?

Attitudes to suicide have altered slightly in many societies in modern times. The prevalent view now is that it does no good to punish further someone who is in such a state of distress, pain, or mental illness that they would try to kill themselves. Attempted suicide is today not a crime in a large number of nations around the world, including the US and the UK, although it is still condemned by most religions.

When did the first pro-euthanasia groups form?

In the early 20th century, a number of books, papers, and discussions about euthanasia started to flourish, leading to the establishment of the first organizations dedicated to the legalization of euthanasia. The Voluntary Euthanasia Legalisation Society was founded in 1935 in the UK by Dr. C. Killick Millard. The society succeeded in introducing a bill into the British Parliament in 1935. However, this failed to become law the following year. In 1938, the Euthanasia Society of America was formed by Charles Francis Potter. However, the attempts of these early euthanasia groups to create changes in the law and to spark public debate did not succeed.

What was the T4 Program?

In 1939, the Aktion T4 program was started in Germany by the Nazi Party, which was in power at the time. It was promoted as euthanasia and mercy killing of people who had, as the Nazis described, "lives unworthy of life." Nazi officials saw major economic benefits in ridding the state of those it

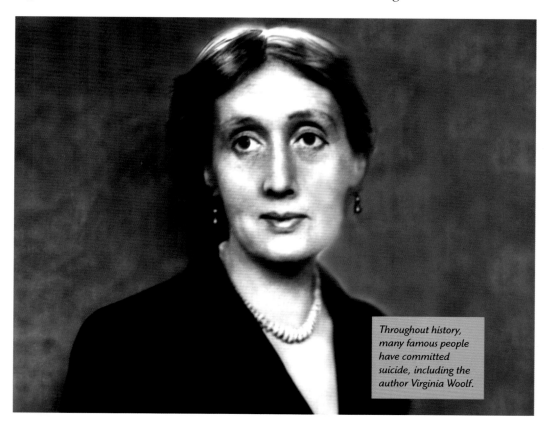

Throughout history, many famous people have committed suicide, including the author Virginia Woolf.

Dr. Karl Brandt at his trial for crimes against humanity after World War II. As Reich Commissioner for Sanitation and Health, he participated in the Nazi's T4 program.

claimed led "burdensome lives" and were "useless eaters." The program was first aimed at children with birth defects but it was later extended to the incurably ill, people with physical and mental disabilities, and the elderly. People, who had no say in the decision, were selected by medical teams and then killed, first by starvation or an injection of drugs, and, later, in poison gas chambers. Some 70,000 people were killed by the program before 1941 and an estimated further 130,000 were killed before the end of World War II (1939–1945).

DEBATE—Was the T4 program euthanasia?

- Yes. The T4 program is an example of what happens when involuntary euthanasia is backed by a government on a large scale. The danger of this occurring again concerns many opposed to legalizing any sort of euthanasia.

- No. Hitler's T4 program wasn't euthanasia as is meant today. Patients were not selected for medical or humane reasons: it was about saving money and the Nazi's political views about cleansing the Ayran race of undesirables.

Why has euthanasia become a major issue in recent years?

Great advances in medical science and public health now enable people to live far longer lives, on average, than in the past. Life expectancy around the world has doubled in the last 250 years. A person can now expect to live for an average of 67 years, and, in wealthier nations, people can live, on average, well into their seventies and eighties. As people live to an older age, there are increased chances that they may become exposed to certain diseases and these can result in long, disabling, and painful illnesses. Further medical advances, including the development of medicines and machines such as respirators, now make it possible to keep people alive despite these serious illnesses. In many cases, a person would not be able to survive without the help of these medicines and machines. These developments have helped to fuel a growing euthanasia debate in countries with rapidly aging populations where health topics are of increasing interest. Some people see the prolonging of a person's life by medicines and machines as degrading and inhuman. Campaign groups on both sides have also helped to heighten the debate (see pages 44–49).

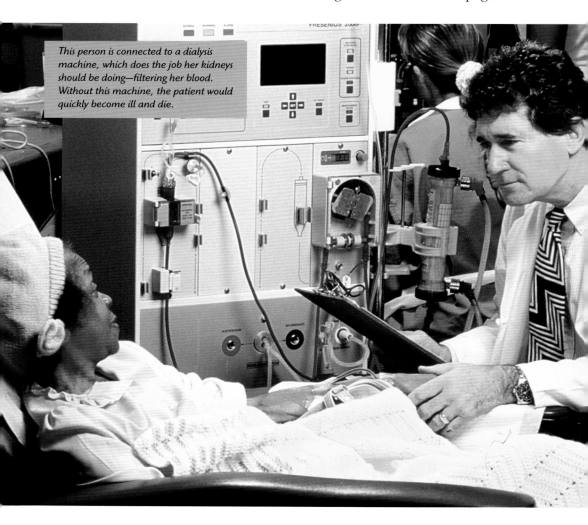

This person is connected to a dialysis machine, which does the job her kidneys should be doing—filtering her blood. Without this machine, the patient would quickly become ill and die.

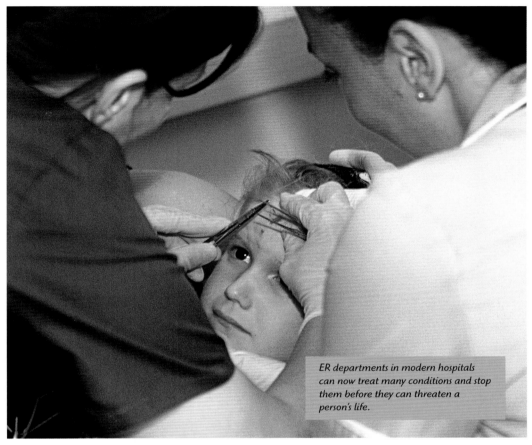

ER departments in modern hospitals can now treat many conditions and stop them before they can threaten a person's life.

Do people today have an absolute right to life?

In 1948, the United Nations, an organization of countries established after World War II, produced the Universal Declaration of Human Rights. Article 3 of the Declaration states that "Everyone has the right to life, liberty, and security of person." The fundamental right to life is found in the laws and documents of many nations. In the United Kingdom, for example, the Human Rights Act passed in 1998 states "Everyone's right to life shall be protected by law. No one shall be deprived of his life intentionally." The Human Rights Act does, however, make exceptions for capital punishment and self-defense.

While these and other documents appear to offer a right to life, this might not be absolute in practice. The level of medical care resources in almost all countries is not bottomless and is often outweighed by the demand from ever increasing numbers of patients. Not everyone can receive all the medical care their condition requires and sometimes tough decisions have to be made about where medical resources go. In addition, patients in many countries have a right to refuse medical treatments and to make the decision not to remain alive by being connected to life-support machines. One anti-euthanasia group, the IAETF, has stated that, "Insistence, against the patient's wishes, that death be postponed by every means available is contrary to law and practice."

What Are The Arguments For Euthanasia?

People wish to die for a wide range of reasons. Advocates of euthanasia feel that some of these reasons, such as being in constant, unbearable pain or being just days or weeks away from death because of an untreatable and incurable illness, are valid reasons for euthanasia to occur.

Ludwig Minelli is a lawyer who set up the Swiss organization Dignitas, which assists people in committing suicide (see page 43).

MOST SUPPORTERS OF euthanasia believe that very severely ill or dying patients should have the right to request that their life be ended. A frequently given example is of people suffering from a terminal illness for which there is no known cure. In the early stages of such an illness, people may have a relatively good quality of life. As the illness progresses, however, they may fear the suffering, the dependency on others, and the loss of control that their situation might bring. If someone is merely weeks away from dying and there is no possible cure, why can't they be given the chance to choose the exact moment and manner of their death?

Shouldn't we show mercy?

Euthanasia cases are sometimes called "mercy killings" in the media—a name that highlights an important argument. We live in a civilized society where every effort is made to give as high a

Christiaan Barnard, a supporter of euthanasia, performed the world's first heart transplant in December 1967.

quality of life as possible to many people. Why shouldn't we show mercy, help people who are ill avoid great suffering, and give people as good a death as is possible?

Critics of euthanasia maintain that advances in painkilling medicine mean that most patients, as many as 95 percent, do not suffer pain, but euthanasia activists counter by asking about the remaining 5 percent, some of whom may be in absolute agony? Is it acceptable in a civilized society that we force people who want to die to stay alive in great pain or distress or doesn't it, in a way, show that society can sometimes be cruel?

Dignity in natural death?

"The prime goal of medicine is to alleviate suffering, and not to prolong life... I have never seen any nobility in a patient's thrashing around all night in a sweat-soaked bed, trying to escape from the pain that torments him day and night... To my mind, when the terminally ill patient has reached this stage, the best medical treatment is death."

Source: Pioneering heart surgeon, Christiaan Barnard in his pro-euthanasia book, *Good Life, Good Death*

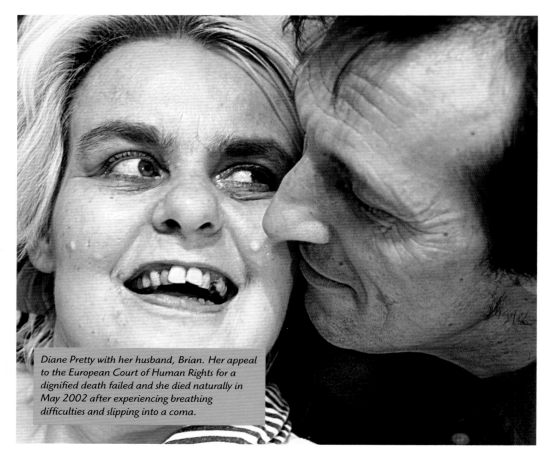

Diane Pretty with her husband, Brian. Her appeal to the European Court of Human Rights for a dignified death failed and she died naturally in May 2002 after experiencing breathing difficulties and slipping into a coma.

Debate—Doesn't euthanasia equal death with dignity?

- Yes. People have a right to say goodbye to their loved ones and not to die in agony. Euthanasia allows a patient to die when and where they want, at the time they choose.

- No. There is no dignity in many of the actual methods used in euthanasia, such as suffocation or inhaling gas.

Shouldn't we allow people to die with dignity?

Some people, like Petta in the story at the front of this book, suffer from what is called a progressive degenerative illness. These tend to be illnesses, such as AIDS, Huntingdon's disease, and multiple sclerosis, in which a patient's condition will get worse and worse over time. Some patients with a progressive degenerative disease fear and experience a gradual but persistent loss of quality of life. They lose the abilities to move, communicate, and be independent and must rely on constant care for all of their bodily functions. For some, the loss of personal dignity is great and they fear that worse is yet to come, including the possibility of becoming unconscious. Shouldn't life be about quality and not quantity? Shouldn't people have the right to die with dignity?

But isn't euthanasia unnatural?

Euthanasia brings a life to an end before natural means have run their course. For some people, it is not as nature intended and this is why it should be considered wrong, a sin, and a crime. Yet, isn't there a case to say that we no longer live our lives as nature intended? Humankind first flourished as nomadic groups of people roaming the land, hunting and gathering food. Today, hundreds of millions live in giant towns and cities. Medical advances have transformed people's lives, sustaining people that in the past would have died at a far younger age. Aren't our longer lives unnatural? And if this is the case, what is wrong with ending lives unnaturally as well?

French teenager Vincent Humbert, shown before the accident that crippled him. Along with his family, Vincent campaigned vigorously for his mother to be allowed to help him to die (see page 50).

US Attorney General John Ashcroft, who made several attempts to overturn the state of Oregon's Death with Dignity Act.

Can euthanasia be properly regulated?

Many supporters of euthanasia believe that it is not that different from many other medical practices and vital decisions made by doctors every day. All other important medical practices are controlled so why should euthanasia be any different?

It can be regulated, many argue, provided it is made legal in a country. It is a known fact that euthanasia and

physician assisted suicide occur in places where they are against the law. These cases often go unreported and cannot be assessed and checked. By making euthanasia legal, it would bring it under the control of the medical profession so that it could be monitored, performed correctly, and to a strict list of rules.

As can be seen from pages 38–43, euthanasia or assisted suicide is practiced under the law in just a handful

Karen Ann Quinlan

A landmark court case in the euthanasia debate occurred in 1976. Karen Ann Quinlan lay in a coma and was dependant upon a mechanical respirator for her survival. Her parents asked doctors to remove the respirator and let Karen die a natural death. The doctors refused and the case went to court. The Quinlans were successful in persuading the court that the doctors' actions infringed on the patient's rights to refuse medical treatment. In agreeing with Karen's parents, the court decided that the rights of the patient overruled medical ethics. In a twist of fate, however, when Karen was removed from the respirator, she continued to breathe and remained in a coma for nearly 10 years, before dying from pneumonia in 1985.

of countries throughout the world. Supporters of euthanasia argue that in these countries, there has been no massive increase in the numbers of people rushing to die. In the state of Oregon, for example, around 130 people have asked for and received physician assisted suicide in the five years since it was legalized. In each case, strict guidelines and safeguards were followed to prevent misuse of the law and to make sure that the person communicated clearly and repeatedly their desire to end their life. In most of these cases, a patient and their medical records were carefully analyzed and second medical opinions sought before any action was taken. There was often a "cooling off" period in which the patient had the right to change their mind.

Pro–euthanasia supporters hand in a petition to the Prime Minister at 10 Downing Street, London.

What about patients who are unable to choose?

The right to choose is considered a powerful part of the argument for euthanasia and assisted suicide, but for some people this is not an option. It is possible for people to suffer severe brain injury through an accident or illness. They can fall into a deep coma, in which doctors and specialists can find no sign of upper brain activity—the part of the brain in which it is believed consciousness, thinking, communication, and understanding occur. This is called a persistent or permanent vegetative state (PVS) and with life-support machines, it is possible to keep a PVS patient alive for

DEBATE—Should euthanasia be an option for people in PVS?

- Yes. A person in a genuine PVS has no chance of recovery. They are technically alive, but what sort of life is it when they are not aware of anything around them? Should the parents of PVS victims have to go through many years of grief without an end?

- No. A person in a PVS is still a person. There have been a number of cases where someone in what was thought to be a PVS has come out of that state. While there is hope of a recovery, it is simply unacceptable to terminate life.

many years. However, many people wonder whether it is right to do so, believing that if the parents and family members agree, euthanasia should be an option in such cases.

Does public opinion support euthanasia?

Many opinion polls taken in a number of countries indicate that the majority of the public support euthanasia or assisted suicide in certain clearly defined cases. In the US, for example, opinion polls show that support for legalizing voluntary euthanasia grew from 37 percent in 1947 to 61 percent in 1999. In the UK, opinion polls during the late 1990s showed public support for certain cases of euthanasia at around 80 percent.

Anthony Bland

17-year-old Anthony Bland went to see a soccer semifinal at the Hillsborough stadium, Sheffield, UK, in 1989 when disaster struck. A human stampede caused 95 deaths. In the disaster, Anthony suffered a severe crushed chest injury which led to brain damage. Despite intense medical efforts he lapsed into a PVS. His parents believed their son would not want to be kept alive in such a state and they were supported by doctors at Airedale Hospital where he was being treated. After a lengthy court battle, doctors were allowed to withdraw water and artificial nutrition to hasten his death.

Tributes are left outside the Hillsborough stadium in the UK following the disaster that eventually claimed Anthony Bland's life.

What Are The Arguments Against Euthanasia?

Opponents to euthanasia come from all walks of life and their reasons for opposing euthanasia are just as varied. For example, some feel that legalizing it would be the start of an increasing disregard for life, while others fear it would create pressure on severely ill and elderly people to end their lives.

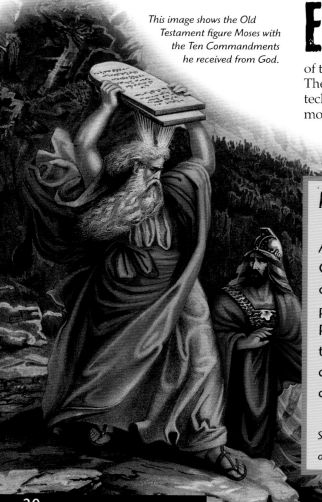

This image shows the Old Testament figure Moses with the Ten Commandments he received from God.

EUTHANASIA IS OFTEN portrayed as the only alternative to suffering a painful, undignified death, but critics of this view say this is far from the truth. They argue that advances in painkilling techniques and drugs mean that in many more cases than in the past, patients can be given a peaceful and painless final period of their lives.

An easy death?

A study of physician assisted suicide in Oregon showed that in seven percent of cases, there were technical problems or unexpected side effects. Patients either took longer to die than expected or, in six percent of cases, woke from a drug–induced coma that was supposed to be fatal.

Sources: BBC News, *New England Journal of Medicine*

In a 1980 address, Pope John Paul II stated, "Nothing and no one can in any way permit the killing of an innocent human being."

Critics also state that euthanasia does not always offer a good, easy, or dignified death. On occasion, complications do happen. In some cases, for instance, people have been known to react to a lethal injection with violent shakes of their body and muscles. These can give anything but the appearance of a calm and peaceful death, and can cause great distress to friends and family who may be present at the time.

Is euthanasia against religious teachings?

Many religions hold that human life is sacred and granted by God or some other force higher than human beings. This viewpoint is found in the teachings of many of the world's major religions, including the Christian, Jewish, and Islamic faiths. In the Christian Bible, for instance, "Thou shalt not kill" is one of God's Ten Commandments, while the holy book of Islam, the Qur'an, instructs Muslims to, "Destroy not yourselves. Surely Allah is ever merciful to you." Dr. Rachamin Melamed-Cohen wrote in 2002 that, "The message of Judaism is that one must struggle until the last breath of life. Until the last moment, one has to live and rejoice and give thanks to the Creator." Some religions even believe that suffering is a part of life and may cleanse a person and bring them closer to God. For example, the Roman Catholic leader Pope John Paul II, has stated that, "It is suffering, more than anything else, which clears the way for the grace which transforms human souls."

Anti-euthanasia protesters outside a clinic in the US.

DEBATE—Are religious arguments relevant?

- Yes. They are the ultimate code of conduct and show a way to live life that is followed by billions of people. You cannot ignore what so many people think.

- No. Religious documents such as the Bible were written such a long time ago, long before medical science had reached this state. They are no longer relevant and many people do not follow them.

Do people change their mind about ending their own lives?

Yes. There have been a number of occasions where people who considered euthanasia or assisted suicide, went on to prosper and lead happy, worthwhile lives. A Canadian medical study of 168 terminally ill cancer patients, published in the medical journal, *The Lancet*, showed that a large number of the patients frequently changed their minds about whether they wanted to live or die. Anti-euthanasia groups fear that patients could have asked for death when they were at an extremely low emotional point. If they had waited even a few days, they would have made a completely different decision.

What about mistakes in judgment?

Medical science may have advanced greatly, but much is still unknown about the human body and how it works. Some patients recover miraculously, while others are victims of honest mistakes made about their condition. A study published in the *British Medical Journal* in 1996 showed that out of 40 patients thought to be in a PVS by doctors, 17 were later found to be aware and able to express simple wishes. A patient believing they had no hope of a cure or had just weeks to live could be tempted into euthanasia even though their condition was not as severe as they thought. If euthanasia was legal, anti-euthanasia activists argue, then how many of these people would die unnecessarily?

Error in judgment

A pathologist in Australia says a woman who took her own life because she thought she had cancer didn't have the disease when she died. A postmortem examination did find evidence that Nancy Crick had suffered from previous bouts of cancer, but that these had been cleared up by surgery. The 69-year-old took her own life with an overdose of drugs surrounded by supporters and euthanasia activists.

Sources: ABC, *The Age*, Newsweekly

Dr. Philip Nitschke has developed several instruments for aiding in euthanasia and assisted suicide cases. He advised Nancy Crick before she committed suicide.

Difficult for doctors?

The American Medical Association's (AMA) official view is that "Physician assisted suicide is fundamentally incompatible with the physician's role as healer, would be difficult or impossible to control and would pose serious societal risks."

Sources: AMA, *The Washington Post*

With medical resources and drugs being expensive and ultimately limited in supply, many seriously ill people feel that they are a financial as well as an emotional burden to the people around them.

Could euthanasia lead to neglect and a loss of trust?

Many doctors are opposed to euthanasia and a key reason is they fear that trust in the medical profession would dwindle as a result of euthanasia being made legal. Would the option of euthanasia being made legal start to mean that less care and attention was paid to terminally ill people as a result? Would research into finding new techniques to care for the terminally ill or to find cures start to decline? For many anti-euthanasia groups, these are worrying questions because they believe the answer to both is yes.

What about unscrupulous practitioners?

Critics of euthanasia fear that making it legal would also make it commonplace and more acceptable in society. This, they argue, could lead to a number of

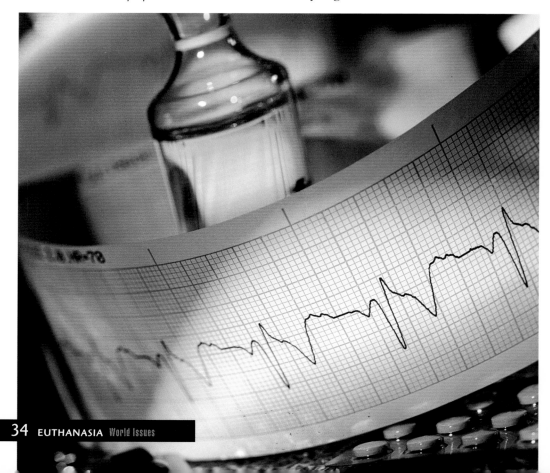

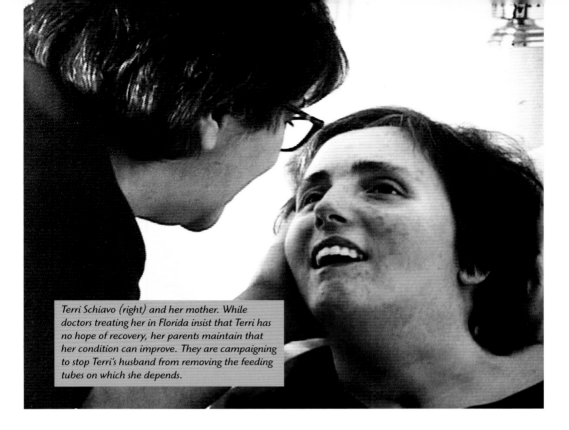

Terri Schiavo (right) and her mother. While doctors treating her in Florida insist that Terri has no hope of recovery, her parents maintain that her condition can improve. They are campaigning to stop Terri's husband from removing the feeding tubes on which she depends.

problems, including the authorities not investigating cases where bad medical practice has taken place. Critics also wonder if it would be impossible to police euthanasia to see if unscrupulous practitioners had taken lives. After all, the key witness, the patient, would be dead and unable to testify.

Could the right to die become the duty to die?

As countries' populations are now growing older and older, the proportion of a nation's budget spent on healthcare and other facilities for the aged and ill is rising dramatically. Healthcare is no longer given freely and without thought; major decisions have to be made on the basis of cost and not all treatment is available to all patients. Keeping someone alive in an intensive care unit costs tens of thousands of dollars. In some countries, families have to bear a proportion of this great cost. Euthanasia, in contrast, is cheap and final.

With financial pressures increasing, critics fear that pressure will mount on doctors to suggest and perform euthanasia on people who are dying of incurable illnesses in order to release resources to patients who have a greater chance of surviving.

Studies have shown how a large number of extremely elderly or severely ill people view themselves as a burden on their families and on society. With rising healthcare costs, would they feel a duty to agree to voluntary euthanasia to stop them from being a burden? Many believe that the right to die, far from becoming one of many options a patient can consider, could become a duty. They fear that it would be impossible to protect patients from pressure to "do the right thing."

Governor of Florida, Jeb Bush. He has been asked to intervene in the case of Terri Schiavo (see page 45) and stop her husband from removing her life support.

UK doctors' concern about euthanasia

According to a UK survey of 986 doctors by Right To Life, 74 percent of them would refuse to help a patient die, while 56 percent believed it would be impossible to set clear rules for legal euthanasia. Almost half said they were concerned about being pressured by families and colleagues.

Source: Reuters

Wouldn't legalizing voluntary euthanasia be the start of a slippery slope?

Could legalizing voluntary euthanasia be the start of a slippery slope toward doctors having the power to take life without a patient's consent? That is the concern of many anti-euthanasia campaigners, some of whom point to the nightmare of Nazi Germany's T4 program (see pages 18–19). They fear that involuntary euthanasia could end up being practiced on the severely disabled, on babies with major birth defects, and on the old who are not threatened with a terminal illness.

Some people criticize euthanasia for, as they see it, putting a lower value on the lives of the seriously ill and disabled by suggesting that an early death is suitable for them. Disability groups, including ALERT and Not Dead Yet, are campaigning fiercely against euthanasia and point out that many severely disabled or ill people continue to live lives which, although difficult, are still rewarding and worthwhile.

Disabled athletes take part in the Winter Paralympics in Salt Lake City. Despite their conditions, they are able to live complete lives, and compete in sports at the highest levels.

DEBATE—Is it impossible to protect patients from pressure?

- Yes. Doctors and families have great influence over vulnerable patients who are weak and in pain. Many patients already consider themselves a burden.

- No. Safeguards could be put in place, including interviews by psychologists and outside opinions, to ensure that a patient makes the decision and isn't unduly influenced.

Where Has Euthanasia Been Performed?

Euthanasia and assisted suicide have been performed in many places around the world, but they are only legal in a handful of states and countries. In the Netherlands, Belgium, Switzerland, and the state of Oregon, laws allow certain cases of voluntary euthanasia or assisted suicide to take place.

Els Borst, the Dutch health minister who oversaw the relaxation of euthanasia laws in her country.

EUTHANASIA HAD OCCURRED in the Netherlands with few court cases for over 20 years, and in 2002, the Dutch government passed a new law. It was quickly followed by a similar law in the neighboring country of Belgium. Euthanasia and assisted suicide remain technically illegal in both countries, but prosecutions will not be brought if doctors follow strict guidelines (see example panel opposite). In 2002, the official figures state that there were 1,882 cases of euthanasia, the majority of which were of people suffering from cancer.

In Belgium, patients must make repeated, voluntary requests to die, be assessed by two separate doctors, and wait a month between the written request and the action. In its first year of operation in Belgium, more than 200 cases of euthanasia and assisted suicide were estimated to have occurred.

Do any US states permit euthanasia?

The state of Oregon introduced the Death With Dignity Act in 1994, but after facing legal challenges, the law wasn't implemented until late 1997. The Death With Dignity Act outlaws euthanasia but

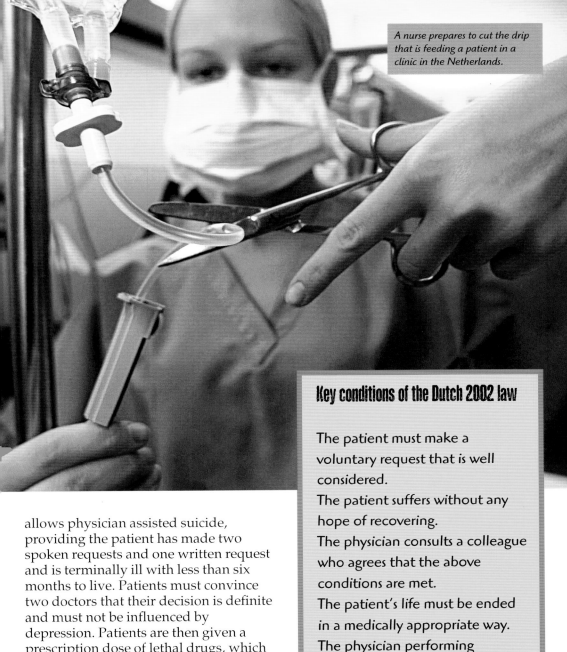

A nurse prepares to cut the drip that is feeding a patient in a clinic in the Netherlands.

allows physician assisted suicide,
providing the patient has made two
spoken requests and one written request
and is terminally ill with less than six
months to live. Patients must convince
two doctors that their decision is definite
and must not be influenced by
depression. Patients are then given a
prescription dose of lethal drugs, which
they must administer themselves. In the
period 1998–2002, 129 of the 42,200
registered deaths in Oregon were as a
result of physician assisted suicide
under the Death With Dignity law. At
the time of writing, the law faces
another challenge from the federal
government's Attorney General.

Key conditions of the Dutch 2002 law

The patient must make a
voluntary request that is well
considered.
The patient suffers without any
hope of recovering.
The physician consults a colleague
who agrees that the above
conditions are met.
The patient's life must be ended
in a medically appropriate way.
The physician performing
euthanasia or assisted suicide must
inform the local medical
examiner.

Sources: ERGO, BBC News

Although he was accused of committing murder, Dr. David Moor was cleared and allowed to continue practicing.

Hungarian Nurse Imprisoned

24-year-old Timea Faludi was sentenced to nine years in prison and banned from nursing for life after being found guilty of the murder of an elderly patient and the attempted killing of six others to relieve them of their pain and suffering. She originally confessed to killing approximately 40 patients but retracted this confession. Euthanasia is illegal in Hungary and hospitals are conducting investigations into how deaths are reported.

Sources: BBC News, *International Herald Tribune*

Where else does euthanasia occur?

There have been a number of instances where euthanasia and assisted suicide have occurred in countries that don't permit them. In some nations, like the Netherlands before its 2002 law, the authorities tended not to prosecute those who committed euthanasia or assisted in a suicide. In many other nations, people have been convicted and imprisoned for their actions. In 2001, after many years of legal battles, Canada's highest court ordered the imprisonment of Robert Latimer for the murder of his handicapped daughter, Tracy, in 1993. Latimer had argued that he had suffocated his daughter out of love and necessity because she was in great pain from her severe cerebral palsy. In the UK, Dr. Nigel Cox was charged with the attempted murder of Lilian Boyes, who had asked him to end her life. He was found guilty but the court gave him a suspended sentence and he was also allowed to continue practicing as a doctor. Another case involved the death in 1998 of George Liddell, an 85-year-old terminally ill cancer patient. His physician, Dr. David Moor, admitted to giving Mr. Liddell a dose of painkillers to ease pain, but which eventually killed him. There have also been incidences of people traveling abroad to take advantage of laws in countries that allow euthanasia or assisted suicide.

What is suicide tourism?

Suicide tourism is when people travel from a country that outlaws euthanasia and assisted suicide to another country that doesn't in order to die.

In January 2003, for example, Englishman Reginald Crew traveled with his wife to Switzerland, where he died from an assisted suicide. In 2000, three foreigners traveled to Zurich to die and, in 2002, that number had risen to 58. Some fear a flood of hundreds, maybe thousands, of people seeking an early death. Euthanasia supporters, however, feel that this is scare-mongering, since Switzerland is alone in allowing nonresidents assisted suicide, and many patients who would like an early death are no longer in a suitable condition to travel.

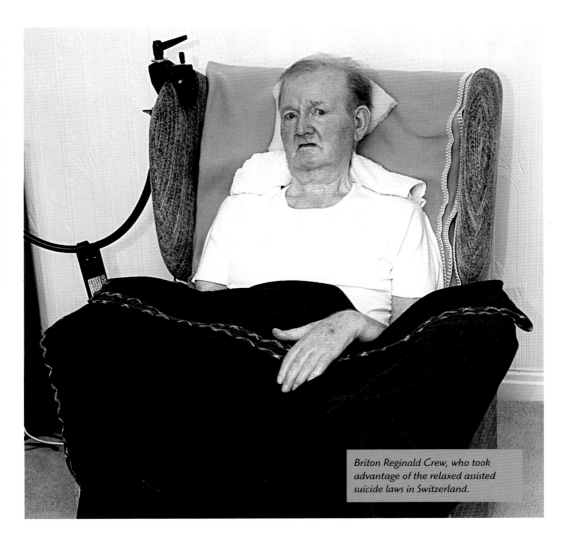

Briton Reginald Crew, who took advantage of the relaxed assisted suicide laws in Switzerland.

Where was euthanasia first made legal?

In Australia, the Northern Territory became the first place in the world to make voluntary euthanasia fully legal in 1996. Under this law, two doctors had to confirm that a patient was terminally ill and suffering unbearable pain. A psychiatrist also had to declare that the patient was not suffering from depression that could be treated. Bob Dent, a terminally ill cancer patient, was the first to die under the law. The lethal injection was administered by a computer, using software developed by Dr. Philip Nitschke, a leading "right to die" campaigner. To operate it, the patient had to answer a series of questions, the final one asking if they wanted to die. If the patient answered "yes," the machine would deliver a fatal dose of drugs.

Only four people died under the law before it was overturned in 1998.

Who is Dr. Kevorkian?

American doctor Jack Kevorkian is the United States' and, possibly, the world's most celebrated proponent of assisted suicide. In the late 1980s, Dr. Kevorkian built a machine that helped people commit suicide by giving them a lethal dose of potassium chloride. In 1990, this machine helped Janet Adkins die. She was the first of over 130 people that Dr. Kevorkian helped to kill themselves in assisted suicide cases. Dr. Kevorkian lost his medical license in the early 1990s and the access to lethal drugs. He switched to using the poisonous gas, carbon monoxide, and was tried for crimes four times without being convicted.

Jack Kevorkian during his trial for second-degree murder.

A still from the video taken by Jack Kevorkian showing him administering the fatal injection to Thomas Youk.

DEBATE—Should suicide tourism be outlawed?

- Yes. It should not be allowed for people who don't live in that country since it could produce a flood of deaths.
- No. A person has to follow and live by the laws of a country he or she visits during their stay there. Why should an exception be made?

Nicknamed "Dr. Death," Kevorkian stepped up his right to death campaign with a case of euthanasia, giving a lethal injection to Thomas Youk in 1998. This action was videotaped and broadcast on US television, provoking great debate. In 1999, Kevorkian was found guilty of second-degree murder and imprisoned for between ten and 25 years.

What is the situation in Switzerland?

Under article 115 of the 1942 Swiss penal code, it is a crime to help a person commit suicide out of "self-seeking" motives, such as receiving money. This has been taken to mean that as long as there are no self-seeking motives, assisted suicide is not a crime. Dignitas is one of several Swiss groups that assist suicides. It has performed more than 150 since the group's formation in 1998.

Applicants, who must be over 18, must fill out forms, provide medical records proving they are terminally ill, severely disabled, or in unbearable pain, and are then interviewed by Dignitas and a Swiss doctor to discuss their case. If approved, patients are given a lethal dose of drugs to take either at home or in an apartment rented by Dignitas in the Swiss city of Zurich. The patient is again asked if they are sure of this act; several people have changed their minds at this stage. If they go ahead with the procedure, they are usually asleep within five minutes, before falling into a coma and then dying. The police are alerted and then carry out a routine investigation.

Who Campaigns For And Against Euthanasia?

There is no one type of person who becomes a supporter for, or a critic of, euthanasia. People of all ages and from all cultures and walks of life are involved in pressure and campaign groups on both sides. In the past 20 years, the number of organizations campaigning on various aspects of the issue has increased greatly.

Anti-euthanasia supporters protest outside a pro-euthanasia meeting.

DOZENS OF PRO- and anti-euthanasia groups campaign by lobbying politicians, publishing books and pamphlets, holding rallies, meetings, and demonstrations and through organized action. For example, Not Dead Yet, an anti-euthanasia group in the United States, has appeared outside pro-euthanasia meetings handing out leaflets. The International Task Force, an anti-euthanasia group, and the Euthanasia Research & Guidance Organization, a pro-euthanasia group, are just two of many organizations that maintain large websites of information in the hope of influencing and recruiting more and more supporters.

AMA continues to oppose euthanasia

The American Medical Association (AMA) at its June 2003 meeting refused to adopt a resolution changing its position of opposing euthanasia. Burke J. Balch from the group National Right To Life paid tribute to campaigners who had met AMA delegates and urged them "not to betray the medical profession's long history of protecting vulnerable life."

Sources: AMA, National Right To Life

The words and actions of individuals facing the euthanasia debate as patients or as family members can carry great weight. In the United States, for instance, a battle between the husband and the parents of a severely brain-damaged woman, Terri Schiavo, over whether she should be kept alive artificially has seen right-to-life groups join forces to campaign with the parents. In contrast, one terminally ill journalist from the UK, Phil Such, attracted publicity when he went on hunger strike for a change in the law banning voluntary euthanasia. Such said, "I have had a great, if rather short, life. Why should this be wrecked by a long, lingering death? I am really proud of my country yet, right at this moment, I wish to God I had been born in Holland or Oregon in the US."

Terri Schiavo's mother is campaigning to keep her daughter alive on a life–support machine.

The actress Susan Sarandon has actively supported euthanasia.

DEBATE—Is euthanasia an issue for religion?

- Yes. By going against important beliefs found in organized religions, pro-euthanasia groups force religious groups to fight back in defense.

- No. Many nonreligious people are against euthanasia and some religious people are pro-euthanasia. The euthanasia debate is not about religion. It is about the law, health, and society.

Who campaigns for and against euthanasia?

The two main sides in the euthanasia debate rarely try to get the other to change their mind. Nearly all of their campaign efforts go into influencing three groups of people: governments and courts, which make and enforce laws; the general public; and doctors and other members of the medical profession. Doctors, particularly, face frequent lobbying and surveys from opposing groups as both sides know that to get their support would greatly influence the public and the government.

Both sides sometimes accuse the other of not reflecting the views of the majority of people and of being funded or flanked by powerful groups. Pro-euthanasia groups are sometimes accused of being in league with private medical companies who might see euthanasia as a way of keeping costs down. Anti-euthanasia groups are sometimes accused of being in the control of religious groups who have a wider set of beliefs than just euthanasia to promote.

Ramon Sampedro was Spain's most outspoken euthanasia campaigner. Although his legal challenge failed, he was able to die through an assisted suicide without implicating anyone in his death.

What successes have anti-euthanasia groups had?

Members of the anti-euthanasia lobby point to the very small number of places in the world that allow euthanasia or assisted suicide as an example of their success. Attempts to pass assisted suicide laws in a number of American states including New Hampshire, California, and Maine have failed, while the 1996 law allowing voluntary euthanasia and assisted suicide in the Northern Territory of Australia was overturned in 1998. After intense campaigning by the pressure group, Right To Life Australia, as well as some church leaders, the federal government passed the Andrews Bill, which reversed the law in the Northern Territory. Only four people died under the law while it was in existence.

Declaration-of-life cards

In the Netherlands, pro-life groups have distributed "declaration-of-life" cards to around 15,000 people. Similar to organ donor cards, these anti-euthanasia cards say "I request that under no circumstances a life-ending treatment be administered because I am of the opinion that people do not have the right to end life."

Source: Telegraph Group Ltd.

Painkilling alternatives

"We already know enough to manage virtually all cases of malignant pain successfully. The widely held belief that pain can be relieved only by doses of morphine so high as to render the patient a zombie is a myth."

Source: Dr. Eric Chevlen, Director of Palliative Care at St. Elizabeth Health Center, Ohio

What successes have pro-euthanasia groups had?

Considering euthanasia was rarely discussed in the past, simply raising awareness of the issue is heralded as a major success by many euthanasia supporters. Many also believe that it is far harder to change the law and the way society acts than to campaign to keep the same laws and attitudes in place. This is why the legalization of euthanasia or assisted suicide, albeit in a tiny handful of places, is still viewed by many supporters as being highly significant. The head of the Dutch Voluntary Euthanasia Society, Dr. Rob Jonquiere, believes that the new Dutch laws introduced have given a major boost to similar efforts in other European countries. "Belgium has followed suit, Luxembourg has been busy and only missed legalization by one or two votes. We know they are busy in France and in the UK."

Dame Cecily Saunders is regarded by many as the founder of modern palliative care.

Is there an alternative?

In some people's view, there is an alternative to both euthanasia and keeping patients alive in intensive care units in hospitals. Known as palliative care, it concentrates on caring not curing and making terminally ill patients' last days alive as comfortable as possible. This can occur in dedicated centers for the terminally ill, known as hospices, in nursing homes, care centers, or at a person's own home. Pain prevention and relief is the priority, but there is also counseling and assistance for the patient, their family, and friends. Critics point out that this care is not available to all; there are nowhere near enough beds for all terminally ill patients, and most hospices are staffed to treat just a small number of the wide range of terminal diseases that people can suffer from. In response, advocates of hospices say that this is more of an issue of financing than a fault with their kind of care.

DEBATE—Is palliative care the answer?

- Yes. Palliative care offers a caring alternative to killing people or leaving them to suffer in the hospital. Greater investment is needed to make even more places available to people suffering from terminal illnesses.

- No. Palliative care only works for terminally ill patients who have a short time to live. What of terminally ill people a number of years away from a natural death or patients with nonterminal illnesses who want to die? It could be made available as another option, but it is not always a valid alternative to euthanasia.

What Will The Future Bring?

No one knows for certain what will happen in the euthanasia debate in the future, but it is likely that campaigns for and against it will become even more intense.

Marie Humbert, who apparently injected sedatives into her son's drip, forcing him into a deep coma.

IN THE UNITED STATES, for example, the situation in Oregon and cases like that of Terri Schiavo are sparking major discussions. Further high-profile cases of individuals suffering and making eloquent cases for a right to choose the time and manner of their death may lead to changes in public opinion and perceptions.

Who was Vincent Humbert?

At the end of 2003, France was undergoing its biggest-ever debate on the topic sparked by the writings and death of Vincent Humbert. Vincent Humbert was a teenager when a car accident in 2000 left him paralyzed, mute, and blind. To write his book, he had to squeeze a journalist's palm with his right thumb, the only part of his body he could move, to select each letter of every word. *I'm Asking For The Right To Die* immediately became a best-seller. It was published in the same week that Marie Humbert, Vincent's mother, put an overdose of sedatives into his drip line. He died two days later. Both Marie Humbert and Dr. Frederic Chaussoy, who switched off Vincent's life-support machine, may face charges of murder. In October 2003, a survey showed that 88 percent of the French population believe the laws must be changed. But many, including the French health minister, Jean-Francois Mattei, were unconvinced, and believe that the law could not resolve what is, in his opinion, "a problem of conscience."

Lord Joel Joffe, who has attempted to introduce euthanasia legislation to the UK.

On the other side, it may not take many cases of unscrupulous doctors performing involuntary euthanasia, which are proven to be against patients' wishes, or of malpractice and painful, botched killing attempts, to harden public opinion and government action against euthanasia. In addition, future advances in medical knowledge may lead to new ways of treating or even curing what were thought irreversible illnesses and conditions.

Whatever happens, both sides will continue to monitor the situation in places that have recently decriminalized euthanasia or assisted suicide, seeking to find further arguments for their case. Whatever their differences, all sides in the euthanasia debate know that it is a complex and vital issue that is not going to go away.

New bill in the UK

In the summer of 2003, a new bill, introduced by Lord Joel Joffe, was debated in the UK Houses of Parliament. The bill would allow a terminally ill adult to ask for medical help to end their life. "This issue has been debated at length in the media and every poll in the last decade shows over 80 percent public support in favor of changing the law," says Lord Joffe. The government maintains that it is listening to the debate but it has no current plans to change the law and the bill is likely to fail.

Sources: *Guardian* newspaper, BBC News

REFERENCE

SELECTED STATISTICS ABOUT THE OREGON DEATH WITH DIGNITY ACT (1998–2002)

	1998	1999	2000	2001	2002	TOTAL
Number of reported assisted suicide deaths	16	27	27	21	38	129
Number of reported lethal prescriptions written	24	33	39	44	58	198
Occasions when doctor present when lethal drugs taken by patient	8	16	14	9	13	60

Average age (1998–2002): 69 years
Gender: Male (55 percent), Female (45 percent)

Six of the 58 patients who received prescriptions in 2002 were alive at the end of the year and 16 died of their illness.

Source: Oregon Death With Dignity Act, Annual Report, 2002

END-OF-LIFE CONCERNS OF PATIENTS DYING UNDER THE OREGON STATE
DEATH WITH DIGNITY ACT

End of life concerns	1998	2001	2002
Losing autonomy	84%	85%	85%
Decreasing ability to participate in activities that make life enjoyable	84%	77%	79%
Losing control of bodily functions	47%	63%	58%
Burden on family, friends, or caregivers	37%	34%	35%
Inadequate pain control	26%	21%	22%
Financial implications of treatment	3%	2%	2%

Source: Oregon Death With Dignity Act, Annual Report, 2002

Statistics on doctors and euthanasia in the Netherlands
Euthanasia or assisted suicide

	1990	1995	2001
Performed it ever	54%	53%	57%
Performed it in previous 24 months	24%	39%	30%
Never performed it but would be willing to do so under certain conditions	34%	35%	32%
Would never perform it but would refer patient to another physician	8%	9%	10%
Would never perform it nor refer patient	4%	3%	1%

Ending of life without a patient's explicit request

	1990	1995	2001
Performed it ever	27%	23%	13%
Performed it in previous 24 months	10%	11%	5%
Never performed it but would be willing to do so under certain conditions	32%	32%	16%
Would never perform it	41%	45%	71%

Source: *The Lancet Online*, June, 2003

Attitudes to euthanasia and assisted suicide in the US

Adults surveyed and asked the following question: "Do you think that the law should allow doctors to comply with the wishes of a dying patient in severe distress who asks to have his or her life ended, or not?"

	1982	1987	1993	1997	2001
Yes, should allow	53%	62%	73%	68%	65%
No, should not allow	34%	32%	24%	27%	29%
Not sure	8%	4%	3%	4%	6%

Source: The HARRIS POLL® #2, January 9, 2002

Survey of UK psychiatrists regarding attitudes to assisted suicide

	Agree	Neutral	Disagree
Assisted suicide should be legal	38%	18%	44%
Assisted suicide not justifiable	43%	17%	40%
Passive suicide not justifiable	9%	8%	83%
Willing to assist suicide	20%	17%	63%

Source: Royal Free Hospital, London and *The Lancet*

Euthanasia rates in the US

In a 1998 study by the Center for Policy Research in Boston, 16 percent of US oncologists (cancer specialists) surveyed admitted to having performed euthanasia.

Source: reprinted from www.bruderhof.com

Euthanasia and assisted suicide in Belgium

In a 1998 survey conducted by researchers from Ghent University and Free University, Brussels, it was concluded that 705 deaths (1.3 percent of the total number of deaths per year) were the result of euthanasia or physician assisted suicide. The survey also estimated that in 5.8 percent of cases (over 3,200 deaths) treatment was withheld with the express intention of ending the patient's life.

In the first year following legalization, there were 203 confirmed euthanasia deaths in Belgium, according to statistics released by the Belgian Federal Ministry For Public Health.

Sources: BBC News, Belgian Federal Ministry For Public Health

Surveys of doctors

A survey of 917 French doctors, reported in September 2003, showed that 43 percent of them believed that "euthanasia should be legalized, as in the Netherlands." Another survey, published in October 2003 in Spain, revealed that 59 percent of 1,057 physicians there were in favor of legislation. Today, at least 85 percent of Dutch physicians support the law on assisted dying that exists in that country. And a poll of 2,700 British nurses, in November 2003, showed that nearly two-thirds wanted the law against euthanasia changed.

Source: World Federation of Right to Die Societies Annual Global Report 2003.

A 2003 survey of some 986 UK doctors by the Opinion Research Business (ORB) found that 74 percent of doctors surveyed would refuse to perform assisted suicide if it were legalised. Some 56 percent felt it impossible to set safe bounds to euthanasia; 37 percent felt it was possible. The survey revealed that 66 percent of doctors considered that the pressure for euthanasia would be lessened if there were more resources for the hospice movement, whereas 22 percent did not agree, and 12 percent were undecided.

Source: Right To Life

US SUICIDE RATES 1990–2001 PER 100,000 POPULATION

Age	1990	1991	1992	1993	1994	1995
0–14	0.4	0.7	0.9	0.9	0.9	0.9
15–24	13.2	13.1	13	13.5	13.8	13.3
25–34	15.2	15.2	14.5	15.1	15.4	15.4
35–44	15.3	14.7	15.1	15.1	15.3	15.2
45–54	14.8	15.5	14.7	14.5	14.4	14.6
55–64	16	15.4	14.8	14.6	13.4	13.3
65–74	17.9	16.9	16.5	16.3	15.3	15.8
75–84	24.9	23.5	22.8	22.3	21.3	20.7
85+	22.2	24	21.9	22.8	23	21.6

Age	1996	1997	1998	1999	2000	2001
0–14	0.8	0.8	0.8	0.6	0.8	0.7
15–24	12	11.4	11.1	10.3	10.4	9.9
25–34	14.5	14.3	13.8	13.5	12.8	12.8
35–44	15.5	15.3	15.4	14.4	14.6	14.7
45–54	14.9	14.7	14.8	14.2	14.6	15.2
55–64	13.7	13.5	13.1	12.4	12.3	13.1
65–74	15	14.4	14.1	13.6	12.6	13.3
75–84	20	19.3	19.7	18.3	17.7	17.4
85+	20.2	20.8	21	19.2	19.4	17.5

Source: American Association of Suicidology

GLOSSARY

ALS Amyotrophic lateral sclerosis. Also known as motor neurone disease or Lou Gehrig's disease, this is a progressive disease that involves muscles wasting away and has no known cure.

antibiotics A chemical substance that kills microorganisms and cures infections in sick people.

assisted suicide Providing the means, through drugs or some other equipment or agent, by which a person can take his or her own life.

autopsy A medical procedure that is performed after a death to determine its cause through examination of various body parts.

bequeath To give money or possessions in a will to another person or organization.

bioethics Study of the moral problems that face modern medicine.

brain damage Injury to the brain causing impairment and loss of certain body functions.

brain death The loss of all brain function, which is believed to be irreversible.

capital punishment The use of execution to kill someone as the consequence of a crime they committed.

coma A prolonged period of unconsciousness from which a patient may or may not recover.

competency The ability of a person to talk or communicate in some other way with a physician and understand the consequences of medical procedures.

coroner The public official whose job it is to investigate any suspicious deaths.

CPR Short for cardiopulmonary resuscitation, this is the massage of a heart that has stopped in order to try to get it working again, without the use of surgery.

decriminalize To reduce or abolish criminal penalties for a particular activity.

double effect When an action has two effects. For instance, giving large amounts of powerful drugs to a patient to relieve pain, knowing that these drugs will also hasten death.

euthanasia Deliberate action to end the life of a dying or seriously ill patient to avoid further suffering.

genocide The deliberate attempts to kill all of the members of a racial, ethnic, or religious group.

hospice An organization that offers comfort care for the dying when medical treatment is no longer expected to cure the disease or prolong life.

human rights The basic rights of all people, which include the right to free speech, shelter, and food.

ICU Short for intensive care unit, this is a medical department that keeps severely ill people alive and monitors their condition.

illegal Something that is against the law.

informed consent A patient giving permission to a doctor to carry out a medical procedure after he or she is made fully aware of the benefits, risks, and any alternatives.

involuntary euthanasia A lethal injection or some other method of causing death that is administered by a doctor to a dying patient without that person having given such a specific request.

legislation A law or laws.

lethal Something that is capable of causing death.

life-sustaining treatment Any treatment that, if stopped, would result in the death of the patient.

living will A document, drawn up while a person is still healthy, that describes how a person would like to be treated by doctors in the event that they become physically or mentally unable to communicate.

lobbying To try to influence the thinking of legislators or other public officials for or against a specific cause.

medical power of attorney Document that allows you to appoint someone else to make decisions about your medical care if you are unable to do so.

murder Unlawfully killing a person who wished to live. It is also referred to as homicide.

palliative care Treatment for the dying that focuses on relieving pain and making the last days of a person's life as comfortable as possible rather than on fighting disease.

passive euthanasia The deliberate disconnection of life support equipment, or stopping any life-sustaining medical procedure, permitting the natural death of the patient.

persistent vegetative state (PVS) A severely brain-damaged person who is in a permanent coma from which it is thought highly unlikely that he or she will ever recover.

physician assisted suicide A doctor providing the lethal drugs with which a dying person may end their life.

prescription A written order, usually prepared by a doctor for the preparation and administration of a medicine or other medical treatment.

pressure group A group that tries to influence public policy, especially laws that affect the particular interests they are concerned with.

right to die Populist general term reflecting a basic belief that any decisions about ending a life should be an individual choice.

slippery slope Theory that allowing one small act, which in itself may not be wrong or illegal, could lead to other similar and wider actions that are.

suicide Killing oneself intentionally.

taboo Something that is forbidden or not acknowledged and discussed.

terminal illness The condition of a sick person for which there is no known cure and which will eventually lead to death.

trauma An accident or incident that affects body or mind.

voluntary euthanasia Giving a severely ill patient a lethal injection or some other life-ending technique that has been clearly requested by the patient.

FURTHER INFORMATION

BOOKS and MAGAZINES

Euthanasia (Opposing Viewpoints),
Katie De Kosta and James D. Torr,
Greenhaven Press 2001
A book containing the key arguments
from both sides of the euthanasia debate
using material including articles,
speeches, and reports to examine
whether euthanasia should be made
legal and what impact that might have.

The Euthanasia Debate edited by Craig
Donellan, Independence Educational
Publishers 1999
A resources book containing reports,
surveys, and newspaper articles from all
sides of the euthanasia debate.

A Right To Die, Richard Walker,
Franklin Watts 1996
A book showing, through dozens of
quotes and real-life examples, a range of
views surrounding euthanasia and
assisted suicide.

*Euthanasia, the Debate over the Right to Die
(Focus on Science and Society)*,
Seamus Cavan, Rosen Publishing Group
2000
This book for young adults is devoted to
the many complexities involved in the
debate over the right to life and the right
to die, including detailed material on
court cases.

WEBSITES

http://www.religioustolerance.org/euth
_wld.htm
A balanced website with information on
the history of euthanasia, the situation in
a number of countries, and the
arguments for and against.

http://www.pbs.org/wgbh/pages/
frontline/kevorkian
An in-depth account of Dr. Jack
Kevorkian's life and actions from the
PBS television channel, complete with
interviews and a timeline of events.

http://www.finalexit.org
Website of the Euthanasia Research &
Guidance Organization (ERGO), a
nonprofit educational corporation based
in Oregon which offers a pro-euthanasia
view on the topic and contains material
and links to a number of the issues it
generates.

http://www.ves.org.uk/index.htm
The home on the Internet of the
Voluntary Euthanasia Society. This
website contains many articles and
news stories about the topic from a
pro-euthanasia viewpoint.

http://www.euthanasia.com
Large and comprehensive website
offering articles, debate topics, and cases
that are presented from an anti-
euthanasia perspective.

http://www.internationaltaskforce.org
Website of the International Task Force
on Euthanasia and Assisted Suicide, an
American-based organization opposing
euthanasia. The website contains many
factsheets and details of specific cases
and campaigns.

ORGANIZATIONS

Compassion in Dying
6312 SW Capitol Hwy, Suite 415
Portland, OR 97239
Tel: 503 221 9556

Death with Dignity National Center
11 Dupont Circle NW, Suite 202
Washington, D.C. 20036
Tel: 202 969 1669

International Task Force on Euthanasia
PO Box 760
Steubenville, OH 43952
Tel: 740 282 3810

Citizens United Resisting Euthanasia
812 Stephen Street
Berkeley Springs, WV 25411
Tel: 304 258 LIFE

Not Dead Yet
Progress CIL
7521 Madison Street
Forest Park, IL 60130
Tel: 708 209 1500

Alert
27 Walpole Street
London SW3 4QS
UK
Tel: +44 20 7730 2800
Email: alert@donoharm.org.uk

Voluntary Euthanasia Society
13 Prince of Wales Terrace
London W8 5PG
UK
Tel: +44 20 7937 7770

The World Federation of Right To Die Societies
PO Box 570
Mill Valley, CA 94942
Email: worldfed@pacbell.net

Christian Medical Fellowship
Partnership House,
157 Waterloo Road,
London SE1 8XN
UK
Tel: +44 20 7928 4694

Friends at the End
11 Westbourne Gardens,
Glasgow G12 9XD
Scotland, UK
Tel: +44 141 334 3287
Email: friendsattheend@beeb.net

EXIT
17 Hart Street
Edinburgh EH1 3RN
Scotland, UK
Tel: +44 131 556 4404

Right To Life
PO Box 26264
London W3 9WF
UK
Tel: +44 20 8992 7657

INDEX